Editor: Kyla Barber
Art Director: Robert Walster
Designer: Diane Thistlethwaite
Illustrator: Teri Gower

First American edition 1998 by Franklin Watts
A Division of Scholastic Inc.
Sherman Turnpike
Danbury, CT 06816

Library of Congress Cataloging-in-Publication Data
    Pluckrose, Henry Arthur.
    Under the ground / Henry Pluckrose.
            p.   cm. —— (Machines at work)
    Includes index.
    Summary: Describes underground areas including subways, bank vaults, and
basements offices as well as the machines used to construct these places, dig tunnels, mine
coal and drill for oil
        ISBN 0-531-14499-2 (lib. bdg.)   0-531-15356-8 (pbk.)
        1. Excavating machinery——Juvenile literature. 2 Underground construction——
Juvenile literature. [1. Excavating machinery. 2. Underground construction. 3. Underground
areas.] I. Title. II. Series: Pluckrose, Henry Arthur. Machines at work.
    TA732.P58   1999
    624.1 '52' 028——dc21
                                                                98—3595
                                                                  CIP
                                                                  AC

MACHINES AT WORK

Under the
Ground

Henry Pluckrose

Franklin Watts®
A Division of Scholastic Inc.
New York   Toronto   London   Auckland   Sydney
Mexico City   New Delhi   Hong Kong
Danbury, Connecticut

Most of the time
we live above ground.
But sometimes
people go below ground.

Maybe they work in the
basement of a tall building.

To get below ground,
they might use stairs
or an escalator.

Basements are often used
to store things safely.

Beneath many banks,
vaults like this one
keep valuable things safe.

Some people go below ground
to catch a subway train.

Subway trains move people quickly from one place to another.

The control room for the
subway system is full of machines.

They control the trains, the signals,
and the destination boards.

Subway trains
travel through tunnels.

Sometimes cars
go through tunnels too.

Tunnels can be cut
through land or under water.

Machines are used to dig tunnels.
First a shaft (a large hole)
is dug in the ground.

Then the machines
that dig the tunnel
are lowered down the shaft.

A tunnel-boring machine cuts (or bores) through the earth.

The tunnel walls are strengthened with iron, steel, and concrete.

A lot happens under the street.
There are tracks, pipes,
cables, and drains.

Machines are used
to dig tunnels for them
and to lay the pipes and cables.

Machines are also used
to carry out repairs underground.

Even farther below our feet,
deep inside the earth,
there are many different
layers of rock.

Some layers contain metals.
Others contain coal.
Rocks and minerals can be mined
by machines under the ground.

Coal is mined
by a cutter,
which breaks the
coal into pieces.

The pieces are
loaded onto
a conveyor belt.

There are layers of rock beneath the ocean too. Sometimes they contain oil.

To reach the oil,
a hole is drilled
from an oil rig.

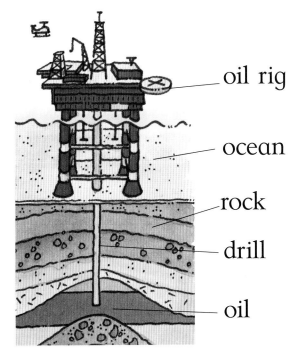

oil rig

ocean

rock

drill

oil

Glossary

basement the part of a building below ground

escalator a moving staircase

basement

mining getting valuable materials from rocks in the ground

oil rig a structure from which people drill for oil

shaft a hole in the ground leading to a mine or tunnel

tunnel a passage under the ground

vault a room with thick walls that stores and protects valuable things

Index

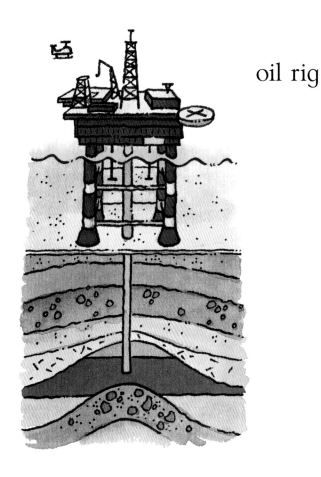

oil rig

tunnel